365

REFLECTIONS

on

Being Single

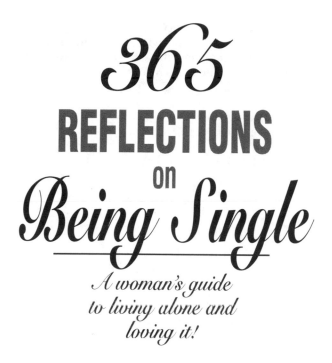

365 REFLECTIONS on Being Single

A woman's guide to living alone and loving it!

Dahlia Porter

Adams Media Corporation
Holbrook, Massachusetts

Published by
Adams Media Corporation
260 Center Street, Holbrook, MA 02343

ISBN: 1-58062-126-0

Printed in Canada

J I H G F E D C B A

Library of Congress Cataloging-in-Publication Data

365 reflections on being single / selected and arranged by Dahlia Porter.
    p.   cm.
  Includes bibliographical references.
  ISBN 1-58062-126-0
  1. Single women–Quotations. 2. Love–Quotations, maximx, etc.
3. Divorce–Quotations, maxims, etc. I. Porter, Dahlia.
II. Title: Three hundred sixty-five reflections on being single.
PN6081.5.A15   1999
305.48'9652–dc21   98-48178
                                   CIP

This book is available at quantity discounts for bulk purchases.
For information, call 1-800-872-5627 (in Massachusetts, 781-767-8100).

Visit our home page at http://www.adamsmedia.com

Contents

Past

Present

Future

for Miss Zambrana
who could have never loved at all

Past

Oh, My Broken Heart

Let's be honest about this up front: There is no quick-and-easy cure for heartbreak. Oh, sure, we've all heard about dozens of supposedly healing concoctions, many containing the base ingredient of Heath Bar Crunch. I once tried a mixture of tequila, cigarettes, and Doritos. Ten doses nightly for a week. Although my hangover and queasy stomach did prove distracting, the attempt did nothing to eradicate my psychic pain.

—**Valerie Frankel**

There are many ways of breaking a heart. Stories are full of hearts broken by love, but what really broke a heart was taking away its dream— whatever that dream might be.

—**Pearl S. Buck**

Pain
Rusts into beauty, too.
I know full well that this is so:
I had a heartbreak long ago.

—**Mary Carolyn Davies**

A queen driven from her throne, naked, in winter snows, like Elizabeth of Hungary, suffers more than she who wanders from a snow-beleaguered hut everyday; the woman who has had the most suffers the most.

—**M. E. W. Sherwood**

Each woman responds to heartbreak differently. There really is no right or wrong—or altogether dignified—way to deal with the pain. You're going to get mad, depressed, even go a little crazy. This is the time to get together with good girlfriends—you can always count on them to trash your ex and convince you that you'll find someone better, soon.

—**Jenny Hayden**

I cried for six weeks—until my friend forced me to go on a blind date. The ego boost snapped me out of my depression.

—**Maureen, in "How to Bounce Back," by Susan Jacoby**

The greater part of our happiness or misery depends on our dispositions and not our circumstances.

—**Martha Washington**

Breaking wedding vows breaks hearts, no matter how many reasons we repeat to ourselves.

—Ellen Sue Stern

The best remedy for a bruised heart is not, as so many people seem to think, repose on a manly bosom. Much more efficacious are honest work, physical activity, and the sudden acquisition of wealth.

—Dorothy Sayers

Is there a cure for a broken heart?
Only time can heal your broken heart, just as only time can heal his broken arms and legs.

—Miss Piggy

I Can't Believe He Left Me . . .

In the twenty-first year of our marriage, as I became happier with my life outside the home, I decided to make peace with my life within it. I suggested to my husband that we call a truce, renew our wedding vows and begin again. He simply walked away—then served me with divorce papers a few days later.

—Carol Connolly

My husband's going through a mid-life crisis. He left me for an *older* woman! What does she have that I don't, except osteoporosis and orthopedic shoes? If he would've waited ten years, I could have given him those.

—**Eileen Finney**

Oh, seek my love, your newer way;
I'll not be left in sorrow.
So long as I have yesterday
Go take your damned tomorrows.

—**Dorothy Parker**

As a general rule, the worst pain comes just before the severing takes place; then for a while . . . there's an inability of the organism (you) to realize it has actually lost and must function without a familiar chunk of itself (him).

—**Irma Kutz**

I admit to indulging in particularly nasty and cathartic man hating, turning *him* into one of *them*, collecting smart-alecky comments from other women, and trading horror stories. This kind of binging is, I truly believe, healthier than an afternoon with Ben and Jerry's ice cream.

—**Louise Bernikow**

At first when I was dumped, I wanted to make him hurt the way I was hurting. But later, I realized that happiness is really the best revenge, so I just focused on the future.

—**Liza, in "How to Bounce Back," by Susan Jacoby**

At some point, separated spouses—no matter how angry they still are—must deal with the practical problems of rearranging their lives.

— **Susan Jacoby**

He may be fat, stupid, and old, but none the less he can condemn the woman's flabby body and menopause and encounter only sympathy if he exchanges her for a younger one.

—**Liv Ullmann**

You know the urge for revenge is a fact of marital life.

—**Jane Smiley**

I am no longer afraid of anger. I find it to be a creative, transforming force; anger is a stage I must go through if I am ever to get what lies beyond.

—**Mary Kaye Medinger**

We had a lot in common, I loved him and he loved him.

—**Shelley Winters**

Loss of Love

I've just pulled out a two-year-old photograph of my wedding. The picture's edges are brown and brittle, from when I tried to burn it, just after my divorce. I had thought torching it would offer some kind of spiritual cleansing, but at the last minute, as the flames licked toward our faces, I extinguish[ed] them. My intense anger began to dissolve into an inexplicable mixture of pity and sentimentality.

—Lynn Woodward

'Tis not love's going that hurt my days, but that it went in little ways.

—**Edna St. Vincent Millay**

Love is the sickness in which recovery is loss.

—**Pam Brown**

When once estrangement has arisen between those who truly love each other, everything seems to widen the breach.

—**Mary Elizabeth Braddon**

Did you ever wake up at the break of day
With your arms around the pillow, where your daddy used to lay.

—**Gertrude "Ma" Rainey**

Love comes into your being like a tidal wave. . . . Sometimes it withdraws like a wave, till there isn't such a thing as a pool left, and every bit of your heart is as dry as seaweed beyond the wave's reach.

—**Phyllis Bottome**

After all, my erstwhile dear,
My no longer cherished,
Need we say it was not love,
Just because it perished?

—**Edna St. Vincent Millay**

Anxiety is love's greatest killer. It makes you feel as
you might when a drowning man holds on to you.
You want to save him, but you know he will
strangle you with his panic.

—**Anaïs Nin**

Never love with all your heart,
It only ends in aching.

—**Countee Cullen**

Oh, life is a glorious cycle of song, a medley of
extemporanea; and love is a thing that can never
go wrong; and I am Maria of Roumania.

—**Dorothy Parker**

Grumbling is the death of love.

—**Marlene Dietrich**

We [Americans] tend not to marry for economic, political, or family reasons. . . . We marry for love and to accentuate, balance out, or mask parts of our own private selves. This is why you sometimes see a reserved accountant married to a blond bombshell or a scientist married to a poet. Perhaps it is no coincidence that the American divorce peak corresponds perfectly with the normal duration of infatuation—two or three years.

—**Helen Fisher**

Falling out of love is very enlightening. For a short while you can see the world with new eyes.

—**Iris Murdoch**

How do you know love is gone? If you said that you would be there at seven and you get there at nine, and he or she has not called the police yet—it's gone.

—**Marlene Dietrich**

Falling out of love is no fun, but the experience is, after all, a fit price to pay for falling into it in the first place. Once you've gone through the mess a few times, it isn't all that terrible, really. No harder than recovering from any other amputation.

—**Irma Kutz**

Love must be learned, and learned again and again. Hate needs no instruction, but waits only to be provoked.

—**Katherine Anne Porter**

For forty-seven years they had been married. How deep back the stubborn, gnarled roots of the quarrel reached, no one could say—but only now, when tending to the needs of others no longer shackled them together, the roots swelled up visible, split the earth between them, and in the tearing shook even the children, long since grown.

—**Tillie Olsen**

Love has gone and left me, and the days are all
    alike.
Eat I must, and sleep I will—and would that night
    were here!
But ah, to lie awake and hear the slow hours strike!
Would that it were day again, with twilight near!

—**Edna St. Vincent Millay**

You start out with one thing, end
up with another, and nothing's
like it used to be, not even the future.

—**Rita Dove**

An excellent way to hasten the falling-out-of-love
process is to phone all your friends—not to weep
but to make them all laugh.

—**Irma Kutz**

All along, one of my worst complaints was his absence from home, and even worse, his absence when he *was* home.

—Sonia Johnson

Love, for both of them, had ceased to be a journey, an adventure, an essay of hope.

—Margaret Drabble

Most women set out to change a man, and when they have changed him they do not like him.

—Marlene Dietrich

Breaking Up

Breaking up is like having a tooth pulled: You don't just do it the minute you get a toothache. You wait until your existence is a living hell, alternative treatment is no longer possible, and getting it yanked seems less painful and scary than keeping it in your mouth another day.

—**Marion Winik**

Divorce is fission after fusion.

—**Rita Mae Brown**

Divorce occurs every thirteen seconds. That's a lot
of *I do's* being undone.

—**Linda Lee Small**

Parting is all we need to know of heaven,
And all we need to know of hell.

—**Emily Dickinson**

Crazy is a word women use again and again
when describing their behavior directly after a
separation. With the exception of those already
enmeshed in a new love affair, most spouses in the
throes of a split feel very, very bad about their lives.

—**Susan Jacoby**

The breakup of a marriage, American style—especially if there's a child involved—is more in the spirit of war than you'd believe possible of a negotiation between two people who once slept side by side. Amiable instances are rumored to exist, although I have personally yet to encounter one.

—**Daphne Merkin**

Somehow, the real moment of parting always precedes the physical act of separation.

—**Princess Marthe Bibesco**

The death of a relationship is painful, but mature people have enough respect for themselves and their partners to cope when love is over. Mature people know how to let go of an unsalvageable relationship, just as they are able to survive crises in a healthy one. Even in their grief, they do not doubt they will love again some day.

—**Brenda Schaeffer**

The reason husbands and wives do not understand each other is because they belong to different sexes.

—**Dorothy Dix**

If you have made mistakes, even serious ones, there is always another chance for you. What we call failure is not the falling down, but the staying down.

—**Mary Pickford**

Kindness and intelligence don't always deliver us from the pitfalls and traps: there are always failures of love, of will, of imagination. There is no way to take the danger out of human relationships.

—**Barbara Grizzuti Harrison**

I don't think marriages break up because of what you do to each other. They break up because of what you must become in order to stay in them.

—**Carol Matthau**

We didn't have a relationship, we had a personality clash.

—**Alice Molloy**

Get your tongue out of my mouth, I'm kissing you goodbye.

—**Cynthia Heimel**

The clearest explanation for the failure of any marriage is that the two people are incompatible— that is, that one is male and the other female.

—**Anna Quindlen**

I Need a Divorce!

We all have our share of troubles. But probably one of the hardest things we do is leave a spouse. From the tundras of Siberia to the jungles of Amazonia, people accept divorce as regrettable although sometimes necessary. . . . Unlike many Westerners, traditional peoples do not make divorce a moral issue. The Mongols of Siberia sum up a common world-wide attitude, "If two individuals cannot get along harmoniously together, they had better live apart."

—**Helen Fisher**

If he felt like working on Sunday morning, there was a no-noise rule. So one summer morning, in yet another room alone with the door closed and headphones on, something settled in me. I wanted my life back. I wanted music. I wanted to laugh freely. I wanted to walk through rooms with the doors open.

—Ann Hood

I do not consider divorce an evil by any means. It is just as much a refuge for women married to brutal men as Canada was to the slaves of brutal masters.

—Susan B. Anthony

The time has come: for us to part . . .
You're like an old shoe, I must throw away
You're just an old has-been: like a worn-out joke.

—Ida Cox

It's idiotic to assume that because a marriage ends,
it's failed.

—**Margaret Mead**

Divorce is only less painful than the need
for divorce.

—**Jane O'Reilly**

I smother in the house in the valley below,
Let me out to the dark, let me go, let me go.

—**Anna Wickham, "Divorce"**

One of the first signs that a woman is in love is
when she divorces her husband.

—**Dolly Parton**

The child in me says, "Hold on," the adult in me
says, "Let go."

—**Harriet Hodgson**

Sometimes, if your own life is to add up, you must subtract yourself from someone else's life. This time comes, I think, whenever you find that the affection or love of someone else can be kept only at the cost of yourself. If you are on the receiving end of much criticism, if the other has nothing but dissatisfaction with you, if you have lost the sense that to be yourself is a good and decent thing, it is time to get out. If love lessens you, if an undeclared war is being carried out in its name, if it is an excuse for destructive demands, if it is painful and joyless, it is time to let the love go and save yourself. You will find another love but never another self.

—**Jo Coudert**

I leave before being left. *I* decide.

—**Brigitte Bardot**

Divorce has been with us just as long as marriage: only recently, though, did it stop being synonymous with failure.

—**Claudia Bowe**

For those who know the value and the exquisite taste of solitary freedom (for one can only be free when alone), the act of leaving is the bravest and most beautiful of all.

—**Isabelle Eberhardt**

You never really know a man until you have divorced him.

—**Zsa Zsa Gabor**

Love, the quest. Marriage, the conquest. Divorce, the inquest.

—**Helen Rowland**

Divorcephobes . . . are not interested only in establishing the provenance of our high divorce rate. They also want to make clear that divorce is, for those it touches, a disaster. When it comes to adults, however, that is a difficult case to make. Again and again, divorce researchers have found that relatively few divorced men and even fewer women harbor any real regret about ending their marriages.

—**Margaret Talbot**

I cannot say what other people should do. I cannot say that divorce is good. I cannot say that it is right. I can say only that my divorce saved me. I weigh ten pounds more and feel hundreds of pounds lighter.

—**Ann Hood**

Finally, I escaped with my life, my humor, and a small percentage of my husband's income. I forged ahead with joy, yet with some lingering sadness.

—**Carol Connolly**

It's delicious. It's scary. It's lonely. But it's right.

—**Merideth Baxter-Birney**

From beyond the horizon shimmers the vista of life-after-divorce: From where I'm standing it looks like nothing less than a paradise.

—**Daphne Merkin**

The divorce will be gayer than the wedding.

—**Colette**

Despite warnings to the contrary, life can be beautiful after divorce. And living well truly is the best revenge.

—**Carol Connolly**

In Retrospect

I have heard that in Persian the verb *to love* means "to have as a friend." Therefore, "I love you" means "I have you as a friend." My ex-husband and I began as friends. We drank wine together and played Trivial Pursuit on opposite teams. I liked him. But my knees never shook when he walked in the door.

—Ann Hood

I'm not upset about my divorce. I'm only upset that I'm not a widow.

—Roseanne Barr

It is ridiculous to think you can spend your entire life with just one person. Three is about the right number. Yes, I imagine three husbands would do it.

—Clare Boothe Luce

I think every woman is entitled to a middle husband she can forget.

—Adela Rogers St. John

I don't believe man is woman's natural enemy. Perhaps his lawyer is.

—Shana Alexander

It is difficult to tell which gives some couples the most happiness, the minister who marries them or the judge who divorces them.

—Mary Wilson Little

One of the few pleasures of a divorce may be getting to tell the world what a jerk your former spouse is.

—**Kathleen Murray**

'Tis better to have loved and lost than never to have been sued.

—**Kin Hubbard**

It is better to remember our love as it was in the springtime.

—**Bess Streeter Aldrich**

Marriage. The beginning and the end are wonderful. The middle part is hell.

—**Enid Bagnold**

Who could know it would be this way—that you enter the country of divorce at your own peril and leave it a changed person?

—**Daphne Merkin**

The question that haunts me most is not "Why did you get divorced?" but "Why did you get married?"

—**Ann Hood**

———

There are some women who become female chauvinists during this stage.

—**Anne Wilson Schaef, of the post-divorce "rage stage"**

———

After years of advising other people on their personal problems, I was stunned by my own divorce. I only wish I had someone to write to for help.

—**Ann Landers**

———

I still love Sean and I understand very clearly, now that time has passed, why things didn't work out between us. I miss certain things about our relationship because I really consider Sean my equal—that's why I married him.

—**Madonna, of her ex-husband Sean Penn**

God, for two people to be able to live together for the rest of their lives is almost unnatural.

—**Jane Fonda**

Love is a fire. But whether it's going to warm your heart or burn down your house, you can never tell.

—**Joan Crawford**

I've been married to one Marxist and one Fascist, and neither one would take the garbage out.

—**Lee Grant**

My ex-husband didn't like dogs and decided we should get a rabbit. But the rabbit never liked him. Once, he was playing on the ground with it, and it bit him on the nose, and he needed a tetanus shot. Anyway, soon after that, we separated, and I got custody of the rabbit . . .

—**Suzanne, in "No More Being Lonely," by Diane Ouding**

I have made it a rule in my life never to regret and never to look back. Regret is an appalling waste of energy. . . . You can't build on it; it's only good for wallowing in.

—**Katherine Mansfield**

Therapists say . . . "second thoughts" are both a natural and desirable part of emotional recovery. You may hate your [ex-]husband, but you also love him. People who never recover from the end of a marriage are those who refuse to admit to any conflicting emotions.

—**Susan Jacoby**

Sleeping with your ex-husband is the purest form of self-defeating behavior from the divorced woman who wants to get on with her life.

—**Sandra Kahn**

All discarded lovers should be given a second chance, but with somebody else.

—**Mae West**

I know what I wish Ralph Nader would investigate next. Marriage. It's not safe—it's not safe at all.

—**Jean Kerr**

If I believed in casual sex, I'd have stayed married.

—**Marsha Doble**

I didn't want to be alone.

—**Hedy Lamarr, after thirteen marriages**

Present

Forgiveness

You can't change what happened between you and your ex-spouse, but you can change your attitude about it. Forgiveness doesn't mean that what your ex did was right or that you condone what he or she did; it simply means that you no longer want to hold a grudge. Forgiveness is not a gift for the other person; it is a purely selfish act that allows you to put the past behind you.

—**Stephanie Marston**

We do not need to press ourselves about forgiveness, but we do need to be willing to feel that gentle tap our higher power sometimes gives to our shoulder. A whisper that says, "You don't have to carry this weight by holding on to hatred about everything that happened in the past."

—**Maureen Brady**

I forgive myself. I did not know then how to know what I knew.

—**Jan Borene**

Forgiveness gives us personal power that we never had when we tried to have power over others. It frees us to do the work we were meant to do. And sometimes, it gives us a way to love someone without pain.

—**Stephanie Abbott**

Forgiveness is the economy of the heart. . . .
Forgiveness saves the expense of anger, the cost
of hatred, the waste of spirits.

—**Hannah More**

Forgiveness is the act of admitting we are like
other people.

—**Christina Baldwin**

I think one should forgive and remember. . . . If you
forgive and forget, in the usual sense, you're just
driving what you remember into the subconscious;
it stays there and festers. But to look, even
regularly, upon what you remember and *know*
you've forgiven is achievement.

—**Faith Baldwin**

Recovery

The conventional wisdom for getting over a breakup is full of breezy suggestion: Get a new haircut! Redecorate your apartment! Join a gym! Yeah, great, but your obligation to yourself involves more than cheerful diversions. Don't just pretty yourself up for your next relationship. Be tough on yourself about your last one.

And *then* watch how rewarding rebound love can be.

—**Dalma Heyn**

You take a handful of rocks and put them in a jar. Then once a week, you take one tiny pebble out of the jar and throw it away. When the jar is empty, why, you'll just about be over your grief. . . . Time alone will do if you're short on rocks.

—**Sharyn McCrumb**

Acceptance is always the first step in healing, as paradoxical as that may seem. We need to work with ourselves and with others from where we actually are now, not from where we would like to be.

—**Molly Young Brown**

A broken heart is what makes life so wonderful five years later, when you see the guy in an elevator and he is fat and smoking a cigar and saying, "Long-time-no-see." If he hadn't broken your heart, you couldn't have that glorious feeling of relief!

—**Phyllis Battelle**

When you can't remember why you're hurt, that's when you're healed.

—**Jane Fonda**

Today I can sit still with my losses, letting appropriate sadness reside in my heart until it is ready to pass on and open me to new friends.

—**Maureen Brady**

Every once in a while I wake up and go, "My God! I was married once. . . ."

—**Madonna**

I have generally followed the conventional wisdom about getting through tough times: keeping busy, not retreating into isolation, not poring over old photographs or making entreating phone calls, not trying to be *friends* when I'd rather be homicide victim and perpetrator.

—**Louise Bernikow**

Mentally and emotionally . . . women who get divorced after a long marriage frequently do much better than men.

—**Maxine Rock**

There will be plenty of time in the future to smile over what was good between you and the silly little man. Keep on telling yourself that what was horrible was all his fault but you were at least half-responsible for everything that was terrific about the relationship. This, of course, may not be true—but then, neither was he.

—**Irma Kutz**

I learned the ultimate truth about heartbreak: It's impossible to cure overnight but, in time—how long is up to you—your wounds will heal.

—**Valerie Frankel**

Real power comes when we stop holding others responsible for our pain, and we take responsibility for all our feelings.

—**Melody Beattie**

It's never too late—never too late to start over,
never too late to be happy.

—Jane Fonda

You may have a fresh start any moment
you choose.

—Mary Pickford

I shall go the way to the open sea,
To the lands I knew before you came,
And the cool clean breezes shall blow from me
The memory of your name.

—Laurence Hope, "The End"

I discovered I always have choices and sometimes
it's only a choice of attitudes.

—Judith Knowlton

The time spent grieving over a man should never
exceed the amount of time you actually spent
with him.

—Rita Rudner

I'm supposed to be a hermit, a loner nursing a broken heart because I lost Robert Taylor . . . My divorce from Taylor was sixteen years ago. If I'd been holding a torch that long by now my arm would have withered.

—**Barbara Stanwyck**

It was wonderful to realize that I—and nobody else—was responsible for the choice to spend that evening there (at a friend's house). I have a *ton* of friends now—I didn't before [my divorce] . . . And I'm enjoying that luxury to an incredible degree. It's all about reconstructing my life.

—**Merideth Baxter-Birney**

Everyone is constantly changing their own past, recalling it, revising it.

—**Margaret Laurence**

We often hear the phrase "when one door shuts, another opens." It means everything has a beginning and an end. When our travels on one path are completed, another path lies ahead.

—Amy E. Dean

Sooner or later it happens to every divorcee. The moment it dawns on you, you can expect to experience a feeling akin to a personal apocalypse. The sky will part, the sun will shine, birds will sing, and music will fill the air. Your life will never be the same. . . . I am speaking of the moment you realize that you're really better off without the husband you lost.

—Marilyn Murray Willison

Courage

Divorce is a foreign country: They do things differently there. If I've learned anything in my sojourn in this strange land, it's that I'm made of tougher stuff than I once thought I was.

—**Daphne Merkin**

I don't know which takes more courage, surviving a lifelong endurance test because you once made a promise or breaking free, disrupting your world.

—**Anne Tyler**

⟜

Courage is the price that life exacts for granting peace.

—**Amelia Earhart**

⟜

Most of us women do manage to summon the courage and dignity to go on with life [after divorce] honestly because deep down we know that we are not only life-givers but we are life-affirmers.

—**Lois Wyse**

You must do the thing you think you cannot do.

—**Eleanor Roosevelt**

No matter how big and soft your bed is, you still have to get out of it.

—**Grace Slick**

People with self-respect have the courage of their mistakes. They know the price of things.

—**Joan Didion**

To gain that which is worth having, it may be necessary to lose everything.

—**Bernadette Devlin**

There is often in people to whom "the worst" has happened an almost transcendent freedom, for they have faced "the worst" and survived it.

—**Carol Pearson**

There are only two ways to approach life—as victim or as gallant fighter.

—**Merle Shain**

Nothing promotes self-confidence more than the knowledge that you are a survivor.

—**Carole Gottleib and**
Carole Huatt

Money

Alimony is one way of compensating women for those financial disabilities aggravated, or caused, by marriage: unequal educational opportunities; unequal employment opportunities; and an unequal division of family responsibilities, with no compensation for the spouse who works in the home. . . . Thus, women should not be cowed into believing that to ask for alimony is to be unliberated, or that their husbands provide alimony out of the largesse of their noble hearts.

—Susan C. Ross

Marry for love and you divorce for money; marry for money and you divorce for love.

—**Anonymous**

What a holler would ensue if people had to pay the minister as much to marry them as they have to pay a lawyer to get them a divorce.

—**Claire Trevor**

No lawyer would leave a wedding contract as vague as most people are doing when they use the word *love*.

—**Susan Wright**

Trust your husband, adore your husband, and get as much as you can in your own name.

—**Joan Rivers**

A superstar duking it out over a five-hundred-dollar TV may seem absurd, but in the world of celebrity divorce, such antics are hardly unusual.

—**Kathleen Murray**

I never took money from anybody in my divorces.
I'm psychopathically independent.

—Lina Basquette

I know there are millions of women who leave a
marriage with no money, no job, no place to live.
That's why I tell women to have money of their
own, or a way to earn it. Because you never know
what's going to happen.

—Joan Lunden

It is easy to be independent when you've got
money. But to be independent when you haven't
got a thing—that's the Lord's test.

—Mahalia Jackson

The courts cannot garnish a father's salary, nor
freeze his account, nor seize his property on behalf
of his children, in our society. Apparently this is
because a kid isn't a car or a couch or a boat.

—June Gordon

Less than a generation ago, alimony was the price that men paid for trading in old wives for newer models.

—**Andrea Axelrod**

A system by which two people make a mistake, one of them keeps paying for it.

—**Peggy Joyce, of alimony**

In Biblical times, a man could have as many wives as he could afford. Just like today.

—**Abigail Van Buren**

You haven't seen someone *really* angry until you've met a female executive who's just learned she has to shell out monthly support payments to a husband she outearns.

—**Andrea Axelrod**

Children and Family

I've done hundreds of interviews with experts on what to expect in divorce, but everything that happens still catches me by surprise. I know I have to watch myself in front of the children. I don't let them hear me say anything negative about Michael. I try not to let them see, in my eyes, in my voice, that I'm hurt or angry. I tell them not to get in the middle, not to take sides, not to be messengers between Michael and me.

—Joan Lunden

In the effort to give good and comforting answers to the young questioners whom we love, we often arrive at good and comforting answers for ourselves.

—Ruth Goode

My mother and father are both speaking to solicitors. I expect they are fighting over who gets custody of me. I will be a tug-of-love child, and my picture will be in the newspapers. I hope my spots clear up before then.

—Sue Townsend

One reason custody fights turn into World War III is that they are waged by the small percentage of divorcing couples who can't agree on anything.

—Jeanie Russell Kasindorf

There is no other closeness in human life like the closeness between a mother and her baby — chronologically, physically and spiritually, they are just a few heartbeats away from being the same person.

—Susan Cheever

This is the reason why mothers are more devoted to their children than fathers: it is that they suffer more in giving them birth and are more certain that they are their own.

—**Aristotle**

How parents should explain their divorce to their children: "I'm sorry, but this suits us, and you're going to have to live with it."

—**Judith Martin**

I believe, as a wage-earning woman, that if I make the great sacrifice of strength and health and even risk my life to have a child, I should certainly not do so if, on some future occasion, the man can say that the child belongs to him by law and he will take it from me and I shall see it only three times a year!

—**Isadora Duncan**

Good mothers know that their relationship with each of their children is like a movable feast, constantly changing and evolving.

—**Sue Woodman**

When one hears the argument that marriage should be indissoluble for the sake of the children, one cannot help wondering if the protagonist is really such a firm friend of childhood, or whether the welfare of his children is merely so much protective coloration for a constitutional and superstitious fear of change.

—**Suzanne LaFollette**

Being a good mother does not call for the same qualities as being a good housewife, and the pressure to be both at the same time may be an insupportable burden.

—**Ann Oakley**

Independence and maturity are unexpected, but not uncommon, benefits of divorce. Children who can see beyond their parents' mistakes and learn from them—as well as forgive them—may ultimately make stronger and more committed marriage partners.

—**Barbara Kantrowitz**

One of the things I've discovered in general about raising kids is that they really don't give a damn if you walked five miles to school. They deal with what's happening now.

—**Patty Duke**

Forget dating. Forget striking a balance between work and family. Most single parents, whether they are divorced, widowed, or single by choice, report that discipline is by far the toughest issue.

—**Jean Callahan**

You've gotten good at being a single mother. As the resident mommy *and* daddy of your household, you have learned how to do it all—make dinner, read to your toddler, help your teenager with his or her calculus homework and fix the broken sink—simultaneously.

—**Muriel L. Whetstone Sims**

Two myths must be shattered: that of the evil stepparent . . . and the myth of instant love, which places unrealistic demands on all members of the blended family. . . . Between the two opposing myths lies reality. The recognition of reality is, I believe, the most important step toward the building of a successful second family.

—Claire Berman

The real killer was when you married the wrong person but had the right children.

—Ann Beattie

It's important for all single parents to remember that not everything that goes wrong . . . is because you live in a single-parent home. Every family has its problems.

—Marge Kennedy

CHILD: You know, that's the only good thing about divorce; you get to sleep with your mother.

—**Clare Boothe Luce**

Yes, single-parent families are different from two-parent families. And urban families are different from rural ones, and families with six kids and a dog are different from one-child, no-pet households. But even if there is only one adult presiding at the dinner table, yours is every bit as much a real family as are the Waltons.

—**Marge Kennedy**

Future

Adjusting to Being Alone

When you look back on your life and try to figure out where you've been and where you are going, when you look at your work, your love affairs, your marriages, your children, your pain, your happiness — when you examine all that closely, what you really find out is that the only person you really go to bed with is yourself.

—**Shirley MacLaine**

I go to bed with a trashy novel and a bag of Doritos.

—**Linda Bird Francke**

Living alone is just like marriage, really, except the person you're trying to get along with is yourself.

—**Elin Schoen**

If you're comfortable with *yourself*, being alone—on Saturday nights, even New Year's Eve—doesn't have to spell disaster.

—**Susan Kleinman**

Adjusting to living alone, as adjusting to anything in life, is best accomplished one step at a time.

—**Lynn Shahan**

No matter how lonely you get or how many birth announcements you receive, the trick is not to get frightened. There's nothing wrong with being alone.

—**Wendy Wasserstein**

When you live alone, you can be sure the person who squeezed the toothpaste tube in the middle wasn't committing a hostile act.

—Ellen Goodman

Solitude is such a potential thing. We hear voices in solitude we never hear in the hurry and turmoil of life; we receive counsels and comforts we get under no other condition . . .

—Amelia E. Barr

Living alone, unlike living with a spouse . . . affords you an unlimited freedom to do what *you* please, to live as *you* like.

—Laura B. Randolf

One of the first things you must do is to accept your aloneness. Then—and this is where self-reliance comes in—you must resolve not to allow it to get the better of you.

—Lynn Shahan

Morning is the constant reawakening that things are now different.

—**Stephanie Ericcson**

I am no beauty, and I'm getting on in years, and I have just about enough money to last me sixty days, and I am terrified of being alone, but I would rather die than sit here and pretend it's okay.

—**Nora Ephron**

For a long time I slept on the left side of the bed, the right side being a vast and empty prairie.

—**Mary Cantwell**

One of the advantages of living alone is that you don't have to wake up on the arm of a loved one.

—**Marion Smith**

Not only do I have the luxury of stretching out diagonally on the bed, I can sleep an extra forty-five minutes in the morning because there's only my alarm clock to wake up to. Also, I've tucked away those slinky negligees (which end up strangling me midsleep).

—**Kathy Miller**

There are days when solitude is a heady wine which intoxicates you with freedom, others when it is a bitter tonic.

—**Colette**

I still feel somehow that things do not really happen to me unless I've told them to him.

—**Anna Quindlen**

Refuse to postpone your dreams simply because you live alone. Live your life fully today—it's the only way to ensure a satisfying tomorrow.

—**Laura B. Randolf**

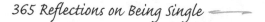

There is no support so strong as the strength that enables one to stand alone.

—**Ellen Glasgow**

Smart women know: Living with the wrong man can be a thousand times lonelier than living with no man at all.

—**Julia Sokol**

For me, the divorce was not difficult. I had been living in loneliness for years by the time my marriage ended, so being alone felt uplifting, free.

—**Ann Hood**

Transform your loneliness into something of value to you. . . . Use it as an opportunity to know yourself better, to gauge your thoughts, feelings, and perceptions. Look upon lonely times as opportunities for personal growth. . . .

—**Lynn Shahan**

I don't like to be labeled as lonely just because I am alone.

—**Delta Burke**

It is not only possible but can be desirable to deal with the anxiety of solitary living and create a life alone that is both rich and fulfilling.

—**Laura B. Randolf**

I would rather be by myself at home than with a man whose company I did not enjoy.

—**Stephanie Zimbalist**

I used to believe that anything was better than nothing. Now I know that sometimes nothing is better.

—**Glenda Jackson**

People who live alone most happily seem to be those whose independence is joined with a sense of purpose.

—**Lynn Shahan**

Living alone . . . can be a time of unparalleled freedom, self-discovery—and just plain fun.

—Laura B. Randolf

⟶

When time alone is not what I want, it may be what I need.

—Carol Slade

⟶

I'd just gotten divorced and moved to Washington, where I knew almost nobody. So I said to myself, "Force yourself." I went to a Fourth of July concert, alone, on the Capital steps and met two guys, one of them just my type. I think if you're alone, you have to reach out. Also you have to put yourself in a place somebody might find you. Hardly anyone will bang on your front door.

—Susie, in "No more being lonely," by Diane Ouding

I know you won't believe me—I've spit at people who said it to me—but I actually feel stronger because of this period in my life.

—**Louise Bernikow**

I wonder if living alone makes one more alive. No precious energy goes in disagreement or compromise. No need to augment others, there is just yourself, just truth—a morsel—and you.

—**Florida Scott-Maxwell**

Independence: I Have Myself and I Don't Need Him

It is well to remember that none of us depends entirely on another for our happiness, although we may think we do. It is not the person we love who is responsible for our depth of feeling. This feeling is part of ourselves, it is our capacity for love and it stays with us despite misfortune.

—Claire Weekes

I don't need a man to rectify my existence. The most profound relationship we'll ever have is the one with ourselves.

—**Shirley MacLaine**

Love yourself first and everything else falls into line. You really have to love yourself to get anything done in this world.

—**Lucille Ball**

There's a school of thought that it really is not very interesting whether a woman is married or not.

—**Diane Sawyer**

Now I know how to change a lightbulb, use a screwdriver, and fix a washing machine when it overflows.

—**Ellen Sue Stern**

To me that's what being liberated is really about—not being defined by one's relationships with men, but still being able to appreciate them on their own terms.

—**Julia Louise Dreyfus**

It saddens me to become once again an independent woman. It was a deep joy to depend on his insight and guidance.

—**Anaïs Nin**

What we all must realize . . . is that we and we alone are responsible for our own happiness. No one else can or should give us what we need to make us whole. We must learn to cultivate in ourselves the ingredients of a fulfilling life . . . Once we accept that the responsibility and power to change our lives is within us, we can begin the process of creating a life alone that is rich and rewarding.

—**Audrey Chapman, in "Living Alone and Loving It," by Laura B. Randolf**

Realizing that our safety does not reside in anyone else emboldens us to find security within ourselves.

—**Gail Sheehy**

Whatever women do they must do twice as well as men to be thought half as good. Luckily, this is not difficult.

—**Charlotte Whitton**

Take your life into your own hands and what happens? A terrible thing; no one to blame.

—**Erica Jong**

Attitude is everything. We've come a very long way since women without men were social pariahs and legal nonentities. I exist. Partnered or not, I have a life. I haven't lost my looks, talent, . . . teeth, friends, funny bone . . .

—**Louise Bernikow**

A woman without a man is like a fish without a bicycle.

—**Gloria Steinem**

I have a lot of friends who are bringing up their children alone. Men are not a necessity. You don't need them to live. You don't have to have them to survive.

—**Cher**

One need not be married to achieve status.

—**Miss Piggy, when asked about her marital status**

Power is the ability to see yourself through your own eyes and not through the eyes of others.

—**Lynn V. Andrews**

I have no wish for a second husband. I had enough of the first. I like to have my own way—to lie down mistress, and get up master.

—**Susanna Moodie**

single (Again!)

You don't have to debate your every decision with a critical detractor; there's no one around to constantly remind you which of your habits make others insane. You don't have to cook if you don't want to . . . You can decorate eccentrically . . . Overall, it's a relatively painless way of life.

—**Merrill Markoe**

Speaking from experience, being single is an ideal opportunity to revel in the joys of freedom, indulge yourself, *grow*.

—**Kathy Miller**

The joys of being single are powerful ones . . .

—**Lesley Dormen**

Uncoupled, I'm free to find my own rhythm. When do I really like to get up or go to sleep, have meals, stay in, go out? Our life together was a compromise between his way and mine. Now I've had a chance to rediscover my own selfish preferences.

—**Louise Bernikow**

The biggest difference, I've learned, between experiencing single life at 21 and again in your thirties is the baggage you've picked up.

—**Joyce Maynard**

You have the chance to focus on *yourself,* to solidify your identity without the undue influence of some[one] . . . you're eager to please.

—**Sara Nelson**

I don't view being single as sort of a waiting period between marriages. For me it is a genuine alternative to marriage. I am quite happily single.

—**Cybil Shepard**

A woman needs a man like a fish needs a net.

—**Cynthia Heimel**

Living single gives us an opportunity to define ourselves boldly and on our own terms . . .

—**Lesley Dormen**

It isn't pathetic anymore to be single. As a friend of mine had the wit to reply when someone asked if she were married, "Good God, no, are *you*?" As much as anything, an unmarried person nowadays is the object of envy.

—**Jane Howard**

Dating and Romance: Take Two

Divorce was the hardest thing you've ever done. Now that you're dating—no longer part of that snug, self-contained unit known as a couple—you feel both uncertainty and déjà vu. You've asked yourself most of these questions before: Who pays? What will you talk about? What about sex? What about the kids? And, where, oh, where, will you meet him?

—Lesley Dormen

When a divorced woman reenters the world of dating and romance, she's likely to feel as if she has entered a time warp.

—Lesley Dormen

✐

I remember my pre-relationship dating days as casual and carefree: You'd meet someone once, he'd ask you out, you'd throw on a pair of jeans and go. Nights were cheap; where you went was not impressive or important. . . . But like a guy just out of jail, I discovered that society can change a lot while you're out of circulation.

—Ellen Welty

✐

As someone with virtually no interest in the "mom" part of you, he's the perfect antidote for all those years you've spent feeling like nothing *but* a mom.

—Joyce Maynard, of dating after divorce

✐

In some respect, dating after divorce is your worst nightmare come true: you get to be a teenager. Again.

—Lesley Dormen

I was married at 23 and, after years of struggle, divorced twelve years later. So I found myself, at 35, living on my own with three children in a medium-size New Hampshire town and feeling . . . the way I had when I was 13, standing on the sidelines at a dance, when the band was playing "Try a Little Tenderness" and everybody seemed to have a partner but me.

—Joyce Maynard

Friends would say, "Why did you let him into your apartment if you didn't like him?" "I don't know, I was tired," I would answer. The truth was, I hadn't been able to remember how to handle things at the door: I had some vague (mistaken) memory that men politely saw you inside and then promptly left if you did not offer them anything.

—Ellen Welty

For many divorced women, the real challenge begins once they find a man to date.

—Claudia Bowe

You're way past grief now. You're at fear. See . . . there you are in the mirror. Looking good. Feeling nauseated. Will he think you're pretty? Will he like you? Will *you* like *him*?

—Lesley Dormen, of dating
after divorce

Cynics would say . . . that rebound romance is but a scab that temporarily covers a deep wound—a wound that only time, not love, can heal. I think they're wrong. Moving on successfully has more to do with guts than time.

—Dalma Heyn

If the first time I was looking for a good catch, the second time I wanted a good catcher.

—Shelby Hearon

Whenever I date a guy, I think, is this the man I want my children to spend their weekend with?

—Rita Rudner

After the breakup of my relationship, I decided that not only would I flirt, but my clothes would flirt for me. I packed up my long flowing skirts, massive cardigans, and precious little flats. And I went shopping: short skirts, high heels, black stockings. I was audacious right down to my new lipstick: It was called Outrageous.

—**Ellen Welty**

Having the renewed courage to seek opportunity is really what you've been working toward . . . Even during those dark hours when you reached toward the heavens and swore you would never date again, weren't you secretly longing for the chance to get close to another human being? To do so, you have to start feeling better about this new stage of life and move on. Lifting yourself out of heartbreak pain will give the emotional freedom.

—**Valerie Frankel**

Another good thing about going to parties alone: no one assumes that an adequate conversation opener is to ask what your husband does.

—**Ann P. Harris**

What would it be like to be dating [again], friends wonder . . . one is smarter and saucier than the last time around . . .

—Joyce Maynard

⌁

When you ask a guy out, you take the pressure off him and up your intrigue quotient in his eyes. But the best part? You're in control. You get to pick and choose when you ask, where you go, and what you do. That means fewer loser nights at the video arcade.

—Malissa Thompson

⌁

I look for a sense of humor, someone with a good ear who's alert to things, someone who's interested in me.

—Merideth Baxter-Birney

⌁

By then I no longer wanted someone who passed all of society's tests for what was desirable; having grown up, having acquired a sense of myself, I wanted someone who passed *mine*.

—Shelby Hearon

Although I've kept my romantic activities to a minimum since I became a single mother, I have had quite a few opportunities to date, flirt, and to fall in (and out) of love.

—**Marilyn Murray Willison**

Everyone needs and wants a little tenderness and there's no reason, really, why you should give up the possibility of romance in your life just because you have kids.

—**Muriel L. Whetstone Sims**

There is really nothing like a new love interest to make you forget the last one.

—**Valerie Frankel**

Sometimes I think if there was a third sex men wouldn't get so much as a glance from me.

—**Amanda Vail**

Men may come and men may go, but the one constant in life for a single mother is her children.

—**Joyce Maynard**

It's still fun to be single. You just have to be more careful. Your date comes to the door, you say, "I'm sewing this button on my jacket — oops, pricked your finger — I'll get a slide."

—Elayne Boosler

What is a date? A date, at this juncture in history, is any prearranged meeting with a member of the opposite sex toward whom you have indecent intentions. . . . One does not have to sleep with, or even touch, someone who has paid for your meal. All those obligations are hereby rendered null and void, and any man who doesn't think so needs a jab in the kidney.

—Cynthia Heimel

Single tail-end Baby Boomers and Generation Xers are disproving the myth that only lonely hearts and losers frequent bars and look for love through personal ads and dating services. Meeting, dating, and mating in the '90s requires creativity and, as always, a little luck.

—Catherine Walsh

Older woman, younger man! Popular wisdom claims that this particular class of love affair is the most poignant, tender, poetic, exquisite one there is, altogether the choicest on the menu.

—**Doris Lessing**

Understanding the Personals —
What his ad says
    (and the truth)
"Looking for a satisfying relationship."
    (He wants sex.)
"Wants discreet companionship."
    (He wants sex and he's married.)
"Responsible male . . ."
    (He wants sex and he's got a job.)

—**Cindy Garner**

If you're willing to travel, or just super-desperate, the best place in the world to meet unattached men is on the Alaskan pipeline. I'm told that the trek through the frozen tundra is well worth the effort for any woman who wants to know what it feels like to be Victoria Principal.

—**Linda Sunshine**

First the good news. There is sex after divorce, and by most accounts, it is joyful, eye opening, and lusty.

—**Lesley Dormen**

I turned down a date once because I was looking for someone a little closer to the top of the food chain.

—**Judy Tenuta**

Flirting environments are everywhere: everyone is flirting bait. Not that you're looking for that "love reaction" from everyone, but democracy in the intial stages of flirtation opens up every possibility.

—**Dianne Brill**

Men

There are so many kinds of awful men —
One can't avoid them all. She often said
She'd never make the same mistake again:
She always made a new mistake instead.

—Wendy Cope

If men can rule the world, why can't they stop wearing neckties? How intelligent is it to start the day by tying a little noose around your neck?

—**Linda Ellerbee**

Some men break your heart in two,
Some men fawn and flatter,
Some men never look at you,
And that cleans up the matter.

—**Dorothy Parker**

One of my theories is that men love with their eyes; women love with their ears.

—**Zsa Zsa Gabor**

Sometimes I wonder if men and women really suit each other. Perhaps they should live next door and just visit now and then.

—**Katharine Hepburn**

A woman has got to love a bad man once or twice in her life, to be thankful for a good one.

—**Marjorie Kinnan Rawlings**

Women want mediocre men, and men are working hard to become as mediocre as possible.

—**Margaret Mead**

Love is like playing checkers. You have to know which man to move.

—**Jackie "Moms" Mabley**

Bloody men are like bloody buses —
You wait about a year
And as soon as one approaches your stop
Two or three others appear.

—**Wendy Cope**

Why are women . . . so much more interesting to men than men are to women?

—**Virginia Woolf**

Men were made for war. Without it they wandered greyly about, getting under the feet of the women, who were trying to organize the really important things of life.

—**Alice Thomas Ellis**

What's wrong with you men? Would hair stop growing on your chest if you asked directions somewhere?

—**Erma Bombeck**

There is, of course, no reason for the existence of the male sex except that one sometimes needs help with moving the piano.

—**Rebecca West**

Don't accept rides from strange men — and remember that all men are strange as hell.

—**Robin Morgan**

A man's home may seem to be his castle on the outside; inside, it is more often his nursery.

—**Clare Booth Luce**

I wonder why men can get serious at all. They have this delicate long thing hanging outside their bodies, which goes up and down by its own will. If I were a man I would always be laughing at myself.

—**Yoko Ono**

Beware of men who cry. It's true that men who cry are sensitive to and in touch with feelings, but the only feelings they tend to be sensitive to and in touch with are their own.

—**Nora Ephron**

It's not the men in my life, it's the life in my men.

—**Mae West**

When men reach their sixties and retire, they go to pieces. Women go right on cooking.

—**Gail Sheehy**

I never hated a man enough to give him his diamonds back.

—**Zsa Zsa Gabor**

One of the things that politics has taught me is that men are not a reasoned or reasonable sex.

—**Margaret Thatcher**

A girl can wait for the right man to come along, but in the meantime, that still doesn't mean she can't have a wonderful time with all the wrong ones.

—**Cher**

Sex

In fact it's quite ridiculous, the shapes people throw when they get down to it. There are few positions more ridiculous to look at than the positions people adopt when they are together. Limbs everywhere. . . . Sweat flying. Sheets wrecked. Animals and insects fleeing the scene when the going gets rough. Noise? My dear, the evacuation of Dunkirk in World War II was an intellectual discussion compared to it. Once in a while there's silence. Usually afterward. It's called exhaustion.

—**Nell McCafferty**

I don't know what I am, darling. I've tried several varieties of sex. The conventional position makes me claustrophobic. And the others give me either stiff neck or lockjaw.

Tallulah Bankhead

As for the topsy-turvy tangle known as *soixante-neuf*, personally I have always felt it to be madly confusing, like trying to pat your head and rub your stomach at the same time.

—**Helen Lawrenson**

Sex is such a personal thing. Why do we think of sharing it with another person?

—**Lily Tomlin**

Even on the level of simple physical sensation and mood, making love surely resembles having an epileptic fit at least as much as, if not more than, it does eating a meal or conversing with someone.

—**Susan Sontag**

Even a notary would notarize our bed
As you knead me and I rise like bread

—**Anne Sexton**

Really, sex and laughter do go very well together,
and I wondered — and still do — which is the
more important.

—**Hermione Gingold**

Why look at sexual intercourse as penetration? I
have always considered my partner enveloped. I'd
rather make a toast to all the great envelopes of the
world. What say you ladies?

—**Judianne Densen-Gerber**

Sex can no longer be the germ, the seed of fiction.
Sex is an episode, most properly conveyed in an
episodic manner, quickly, often ironically. It is a
bursting forth of only one of the cells in the body
of the omnipotent "I," the one who hopes by
concentration of tone and voice to utter the sound
of reality.

—**Elizabeth Hardwick**

I could hear the lovely, tiny swallowing gulps —
you cover all ages in the sex-play cycle, from
nursing infant to death, in one terrifying swoop of
the sexual plot.

—Jill Robinson

⟵——

We tend to think of the erotic as an easy,
tantalizing sexual arousal. I speak of the erotic as
the deepest life force, a force which moves us
toward living in a fundamental way.

—Audre Lorde

⟵——

If sex and creativity are often seen by dictators as
subversive activities, it's because they lead to the
knowledge that you own your own body (and with
it your own voice), and that's the most
revolutionary insight of all.

—Erica Jong

Tamed as it may be, sexuality remains one of the demonic forces in human consciousness — pushing us at intervals close to taboo and dangerous desires, which range from the impulse to commit sudden arbitrary violence upon another person to the voluptuous yearning for the extinction of one's consciousness, for death itself.

—**Susan Sontag**

Seamed stockings aren't subtle but they certainly do the job. You shouldn't wear them when out with someone you're not prepared to sleep with, since their presence is tantamount to saying, "Hi there, big fellow, please rip my clothes off at your earliest opportunity." If you really want your escort paralytic with lust, stop frequently to adjust the seams.

—**Cynthia Heimel**

You can seduce a man without taking anything off, without even touching him.

—**Rae Dawn Chong**

The important thing in acting is to be able to laugh and cry. If I have to cry, I think of my sex life. If I have to laugh, I think of my sex life.

—**Glenda Jackson**

Once you know what women are like, men get kind of boring. I'm not trying to put them down, I mean I like them sometimes as people, but sexually they're dull.

—**Rita Mae Brown**

Personally, I like sex and don't care what a man thinks of me as long as I get what I want from him — which is usually sex.

—**Valerie Perrine**

You never know a guy until you've tried him in bed. You know more about a guy in one night in bed than you do in months of conversation.

—**Edith Piaf**

I find it extraordinary that a straightforward if inelegant device for ensuring the survival of the species should involve human beings in such emotional turmoil. Does sex have to be taken so seriously?

—**P. D. James**

No man can be friends with a woman he finds attractive. He always wants to have sex with her. Sex is always out there. Friendship is ultimately doomed and that's the end of the story.

—**Nora Ephron**

Easy is an adjective used to describe a woman who has the sexual morals of a man.

—**Nancy Linn-Desmond**

Men reach their sexual peak at eighteen. Women reach theirs at thirty-five. Do you get the feeling that God is playing a practical joke?

—**Rita Rudner**

What does a woman want? She wants what she has been told she ought to want. . . . Orgasm is no proof of anything. Orgasm is proof of orgasm. Someday every woman will have orgasms — like every family has color TV — and we can get on with the real business of life.

—**Erica Jong**

I had the feeling that Pandora's box contained the mysteries of woman's sensuality, so different from man's and for which man's language was inadequate. The language of sex had yet to be invented.

—**Anaïs Nin**

Remarriage

I concluded that I was skilled, however poorly, at only one thing: marriage. And so I set about the business of selling myself and two children to some unsuspecting man who might think me a desirable second-hand mate, a man of good means and disposition willing to support another man's children in some semblance of the style to which they were accustomed. My heart was not in the chase, but I was tired and there was no alternative. I could not afford freedom.

—**Barbara Howar**

I'd marry again if I found a man who had $15 million and would sign over half of it to me before the marriage, and guarantee that he'd be dead within a year.

—**Bette Davis**

The room was filled with people who hadn't talked to each other in years, including the bride and bridegroom.

—**Dorothy Parker, of her second marriage to Alan Campbell**

Well, being divorced is like being hit by a Mack truck. If you live through it, you start looking very carefully to the right and to the left.

—**Jean Kerr**

Look twice before you leap.

—**Charlotte Brontë**

I don't sit around thinking that I'd like to have another husband; only another man would make me think that way.

—**Lauren Bacall**

People keep asking me if I'll marry again. It's as if when you've had one crash you want another.

—**Stephanie Beacham**

I'll try. I'll try, really. I'll try again. The marriage. The baby. The house. The whole damn bore.

—**Anne Stevenson**

Changing husbands is only changing troubles.

—**Kathleen Norris**

Most used husbands come with strings attached and the ghosts of the past are nothing to the tangles of the present.

—**Bettina Arndt**

There is so little difference between husbands you might as well keep the first.

—**Adela Rogers St. John**

I don't care about men. I've given up on them, personally.

—**Marguerite Duras**

As far as I am concerned I would rather spend the rest of my life in prison than marry again.

—George Sand

Whenever you want to marry someone, go have lunch with his ex-wife.

—Shelley Winters

Oh, don't worry about Alan . . . Alan will always land on somebody's feet.

—Dorothy Parker, of her ex-husband the day their divorce became final

You mean apart from my own?

—Zsa Zsa Gabor, when questioned as to the number of husbands she'd had

There is no fury like an ex-wife looking for new lover.

—Cyril Connolly

Actually, I believe in marriage, having done it three times.

> —Joan Collins

Sometimes you fancy egg and chips, sometimes steak and tomatoes.

> —Lesley-Anne Down,
> **explaining her short marriage
> to an Argentinean**

Whenever I get married, I start buying *Gourmet* magazine. I think of it as my own personal bride's disease.

> —Nora Ephron

The grandmother opens the envelope with the letter-opener that Helen's first husband gave her and finds a colored photograph of Helen's second husband and his new wife, Myrna, surrounded by Myrna's children from her first marriage, "Season's Greetings from the Hannibals!"

> —Judith Rascoe

I found myself, avoiding, to some degree, talking about my upcoming marriage with my children.

—**Ann P. Harris**

Because of her background, my mother found dissolution easy, acceptable. My grandfather's five children scored, at last count, thirteen marriages among them. Cousins would refer facetiously, with a certain dark optimism, to their mother's current husband.

—**Marina Rust**

I will never marry again.

—**Barbara Hutton, after her third divorce**

For her fifth wedding, the bride wore black and carried a scotch and soda.

—**Phyllis Battelle, of Barbara Hutton's fifth wedding**

I've been married once on the level, and twice in America.

—Texas Guinan

The woman who remembers her first kiss now has a daughter who can't even remember her first husband.

—Anonymous

Sometime during the move from Chicago to New York, just before Josie moved in with Phillip Neuveville, she took back her maiden name.

—Ann Beattie

I didn't like either of my husbands. Why carry their names around? I don't want to be identified as Mrs. anybody.

—Cher, on changing her
name to Cher

While the remarriage of an ex can be a wrenching ordeal for *you*, think of it as an opportunity to at last make peace with the pain of divorce, a time to heal, grow, and move on.

—Eleanor Berman

Remarriage is an excellent test of how amicable your divorce was.

—Margo Kaufman

I do not want to get divorced again, though I want to remarry. I want to get married right this time—for love and passion and shaky knees. And I want it to last.

—Ann Hood

I always say a girl must get married for love—and just keep on getting married until she finds it.

—Zsa Zsa Gabor

Live and Learn
and Live Again

When a couple decide to divorce, they should inform both sets of parents before having a party and telling all their friends. This is not only courteous but practical. Parents may be very willing to pitch in with comments, criticism and malicious gossip of their own to help the divorce along.

—P. J. O'Rourke

The three "gets"; get a lawyer, get a job, get laid.

> **—Judith Crist, advice to a
> woman contemplating
> divorce**

She always believed in the adage, "Leave them while you're looking good."

> **—Anita Loos**

Truth be told, there is nothing like a divorce to make a Madonna out of a Tammy Wynette.

> **—Daphne Merkin**

In our family we don't divorce our men—we bury them.

> **—Ruth Gordon**

If men acted after marriage as they do during courtship, there would be fewer divorces—and more bankruptcies.

—Frances Rodman

Be careful of whom you marry because divorce is forever.

—Anonymous

A New York divorce is in itself a diploma of virtue. . . .

—Edith Wharton

There is no map for life; unfair things happen . . .

—Elizabeth Glaser

Don't love anything that can't love you back.

—**Noreen Briggs**

Divorce? Never. But murder often!

—**Sybil Thorndike**

He taught me housekeeping; when I divorce I keep the house.

—**Zsa Zsa Gabor**

Bibliography

A. K. Adams. *The Home Book of Humorous Quotations.* New York: Dodd, Mead and Co., 1969.

Abby Adams, comp. *An Uncommon Scold.* New York: Simon and Schuster, 1989.

Andrea Axelrod. "Alimony Today: Do You Know the Rules?" *Cosmopolitan,* April 1991: 216.

Eleanor Berman. "I Don't Want Him, You Can't Have Him—When Your Ex Remarries." *Cosmopolitan,* Oct. 1994:231.

Louise Bernikow. "How to Live Without a Man (For Now)." *Cosmopolitan,* June 1995: 76.

Mary Biggs. *Women's Words: The Columbia Book of Quotations by Women.* New York: Columbia University Press, 1996.

Claudia Bowe. "Everything We Think, Feel, and Do About Divorce." *Cosmopolitan,* Feb. 1992: 199.

Michele Brown and Ann O'Connor. *Hammer and Tongues: The Best of Women's Wit and Humor.* New York: St. Martin' Press, 1986.

Carol Connolly. "I Was Dumped—But I Got My Revenge." *Ladies Home Journal,* May 1992: 112.

Stephen Donadio, Joan Smith, Susan Mesner, and Rebecca Davidson, eds. *The New York Public Library Book of 20th Century American Quotations.* New York: Stonesong Press, 1992.

Lesley Dormen. "Second Chance at Love: a Divorced Woman's Guide to Dating." *Redbook*, Apr. 1992: 50.

Lesley Dormen. "Your Single Life: 6 Ways to Enjoy the Adventure." *Glamour*, April 1995: 254.

Helen Exley. *Love Quotations.* Waterford, UK: Exley Publications, 1992.

Helen E. Fisher. "After All, Maybe It's . . . Biology." *Psychology Today*, March-April 1993: 40.

Rudolf Flesch. *The New Book of Unusual Quotations.* New York: Harper and Row Publishers, 1957.

Valerie Frankel. "Love Recovery." *Mademoiselle*, Sept. 1995: 214.

Gil Friedman. *A Dictionary of Love.* Arcata, CA: Yara Press, 1990.

Susan Ginsberg, ed. *Family Wisdom.* New York: Columbia University Press, 1996.

H. Gordon Havens. *The Dictionary of Love, Marriage, Sex & Romance.* Sarasota, CA: R&E Publishers, 1992.

Jenny Hayden. "What I Did After He Broke My Heart." *Cosmopolitan*, Sept. 1996: 172.

Shelby Hearon. "Making a List and Checking it Twice." *Cosmopolitan*, Feb. 1988: 168.

Dalma Heyn. "Love on the Rebound." *Mademoiselle*, April 1989: 140.

Ann Hood. "My! What a Wonderful Divorce We're Having." *Cosmopolitan*, Oct. 1996: 140.

Susan Jacoby. "Grief and Relief: The Mixed Emotions of Divorce." *Cosmopolitan*, May 1993: 226.

Susan Jacoby. "How to Bounce Back After Being Really Badly Burned." *Cosmopolitan*, April 1997: 242.

Sandra Kahn. "How to Stop Being an Ex-wife . . . and Start Being Yourself." *Cosmopolitan*, Oct. 1990: 240.

Barbara Kantrowitz. "Breaking the Divorce Cycle." *Newsweek*, Jan. 13, 1992: 48.

Jeanie Russel Kasindorf. "Degrees of Separation: The Nasty New Business of Fighting for Child Custody." *New York*, Feb. 28, 1994: 42.

Susan Klienman. "You Can be Single and Live a Rich, Full Life." *Cosmopolitan*, Sept. 1994: 186.

Irma Kutz. "You Can Fall Out of Love." *Cosmopolitan*, March 1995: 136.

Bruce Lansky. *Lovesick: The Best Quotes about Love & Sex*. New York: Meadowbrook Press, 1996.

Jordan L. Linfield and Joseph Krevisky, eds. *Words of Love: Romantic Quotations from Plato to Madonna*. New York: Random House, 1997.

The Macmillian Dictionary of Quotations. New York: Macmillian Publishing Co., 1987.

Rosalie Maggio, comp. *The Beacon Book of Quotations by Women*. Boston: Beacon Press, 1991.

Rosalie Maggio, comp. *The New Beacon Book of Quotations by Women*. Boston: Beacon Press, 1996.

Merrit Malloy and Marsha Rose. *Comedians' Quote Book*. New York: Sterling Publishing Co., 1993.

Merrill Markoe. "Pets and the Single Girl." *Cosmopolitan*, Oct. 1994: 158.

Joyce Maynard. "Single Mother Seeks Love and Romance." *Redbook*, Oct. 1996: 67.

Peter McWilliams and Jean Sedillos, eds. *The Life 101 Quote Book*. Los Angeles: Prelude Press, 1996.

Fred Metcalf. *The Penguin Dictionary of Modern Humorous Quotations*. New York: Viking, 1986.

Kathy Miller. "How to Stay Single Forever." *Cosmopolitan*, Aug. 1996: 86.

Margaret Miner and Hugh Rawson, eds. *The New International Dictionary of Quotations*. New York: Dutton, 1993.

Marianne Espinosa Murphy. "Divorce Stinks: A Judge's View." *Cosmopolitan*, April 1995: 39.

Kathleen Murray. "Odd Couples and Their Odder Divorce Settlements." *Cosmopolitan*, May 1996: 222.

Sara Nelson. "25 Ways to Celebrate Not Having a Boyfriend." *Glamour*, June 1993: 114.

Diane Ouding. "No More Being Lonely: How Some Lively Cosmo Girls Meet Men." *Cosmopolitan*, June 1988: 152.

Elaine Partnow. *The New Quotable Woman*. New York: Facts on File, 1992.

Elaine Partnow. *The Quotable Woman 1800-1975*. Los Angeles: Corwin Books, 1977.

Peter Potter, comp. *All About Love*. New Caanan, CT: William Mulvey, Inc., 1988.

The Quotable Woman. Philadelphia: The Running Press, 1991.

Quotable Women. Philadelphia: Running Press, 1994.

Vicky Jo Radovsky. "Being Single Again Is Scary—and Gorgeous." *Cosmopolitan*, July 1990: 42.

Laura B. Randolf. "Living Alone and Loving It." *Ebony*, June 1988: 60.

The Reader's Digest Treasury of Modern Quotations. New York: Thomas Crowell Co., 1975.

Maxine Rock. "Your Favorite Couple Is Divorcing . . . How to Make the Best of an Awkward Situation." *New Choices for Retirement Living*, April 1992: 42.

Jody L. Rohlena, ed. *Sound Like a Woman*. NY: Penguin Books, 1993.

Marina Rust. "Split Decision." *Vogue*, Feb. 1994: 66.

William Safire and Leonard Safir, eds. *Words of Wisdom*. New York: Simon and Schuster, 1989.

Claire Safran. "Good Morning, Heartache!" *Cosmopolitan*, August 1992: 80.

Ronald B. Schwartz. *The 501 Best and Worst Things Ever Said about Marriage*. New York: Citadel Press, 1995.

Seasons of the Heart: Perennial Wisdom on Moving Through the Cycles of Our Relationships. New York: HarperCollins Publishers, 1993.

Lynn Shahan. "Living Alone and Liking It." *Cosmopolitan*, Dec. 1981: 110.

Ned Sherrin. *The Oxford Dictionary of Humorous Quotations*. Oxford: Oxford University Press, 1995.

Linda Lee Small. "New-Wave Divorce: When You've Got the Money." *Cosmopolitan*, Feb 1990: 92.

Autumn Stephens. *Wild Words from Wild Women*. Berkeley, CA: Conari Press, 1993.

Ellen Sue Stern. *Starting Over: Meditations for Divorced Women*. New York: Dell Publishing, 1995.

Margaret Talbot. "Love, American Style: What the Alarmists about Divorce Don't Get about Idealism in America." *The New Republic*, April 14, 1997: 30.

Tad Tuleja. *Quirky Quotations*. New York: Harmony Books, 1992.

Ellen Welty. "Brave New Girl: How I Learned to Date— Again." *Mademoiselle*, Nov. 1988: 180.

Robin Westen. "A Crash Course in 'Foreign Affairs.'" *Cosmopolitan*, Feb. 1989: 206.

Marilyn Murray Willison. "From the Notebook of a Divorced Woman." *Cosmopolitan*, Feb. 1980: 120.

Marion Winik. "Women Who Love Men Don't Pay Their Parking Tickets." *Cosmopolitan*, Apr. 1994: 136.

Jon Winokur, comp. *A Curmudgeon's Garden of Love.* New York: New American Library, 1989.

Jon Winokur, comp. *True Confessions.* New York: Dutton, 1992.

Women's Wit and Wisdom. Philadelphia: Running Press, 1991.

Lynn Woodward. "Be Careful What You Wish For . . . It Might Come True." *Cosmopolitan*, May 1994: 274.

Susan Wright. "Put Yourself First: He'll Love You For It." *Cosmopolitan*, Jan. 1994: 216.